FORTY ARTISTS

UNDER FORTY

THEODOROS STAMOS.

High Snow—Low Sun, II. (1957.)
Oil. 53 1/2 x 97 1/2.
Gift of the Friends of the
Whitney Museum of American Art.

FORTY ARTISTS UNDER FORTY

FROM THE COLLECTION OF THE

WHITNEY MUSEUM OF AMERICAN ART

Lloyd Goodrich
and Edward Bryant

PUBLISHED FOR THE

WHITNEY MUSEUM OF AMERICAN ART BY

FREDERICK A. PRAEGER, PUBLISHER, NEW YORK

BOOKS THAT MATTER

Published in the United States of America in 1962 by

Frederick A. Praeger, Inc., Publisher

64 University Place, New York 3, N. Y.

Library of Congress Catalog Number: 62-19111

Biographical notes edited by EDWARD BRYANT *Associate Curator, Whitney Museum of American Art*

Designed by Peter Oldenburg. Printed in the United States

of America by the Capital City Press, Inc., Montpelier, Vermont.

Foreword

The young artist in contemporary society embarks on a profession that presents many uncertainties. The essential challenge, of course, is purely artistic: the developing of his personal viewpoint, style and skill—a process that is enough to occupy most of his time and energy. But in addition there are practical problems—getting his work exhibited and sold, making a living out of it—problems that are more acute for the painter and sculptor than for workers in most other arts. Except for a fortunate few, the young artist must go through years before he can live by his creative work alone. Until then, he depends usually on teaching or on employment outside the field of art.

Hence those concerned with contemporary art and artists have always given particular attention to the critical early years—the years that determine whether the individual can survive as an artist, or whether his gift will be lost to the world. In the last quarter-century, foundation grants and fellowships for young artists have increased many times over. The federal government has assisted with the intelligent and well-administered Fulbright program. Dealers' galleries devoted to new talent have multiplied. And museums today are far more hospitable to young artists than they were even twenty-five years ago.

In this evolution the Whitney Museum of American Art has played an active part. Indeed, its activities on behalf of younger artists originated long before the museum itself was founded. In 1915 Gertrude Vanderbilt Whitney, herself an established sculptor, deeply interested in the problems of her fellow workers, formed the Friends of the Young Artists, "to give young artists in this country the opportunity to show their work." One of her innovations was to replace the outworn prize system with a program of purchases—a much more meaningful method of recognition. Out of the Friends, in 1918, grew the Whitney Studio Club, with Juliana Force as director—the liveliest center for the rising generation, where many future leaders had their first chance to exhibit and sell. And out of the Club, in 1930, grew the Museum.

From the beginning, an essential feature of the Museum's policy was to give early recognition to young talent. Its large annual exhibitions of contemporary American art have always included a sizable proportion of new names. But with the constantly growing number of young men and women entering the profession, something more was called for; so in 1957 the Museum commenced a series of "Young America" exhibitions, each presenting thirty artists thirty-five years old or under, represented by several examples, with a catalogue giving biographical information. The aim has been to select individuals who have already produced solid achievements but have not yet attained wide recognition. These "Young America" exhibitions are also shown in other museums throughout the country. From each show purchases have been made for the Whitney's permanent collection.

The Museum has been the beneficiary of several funds devoted largely or entirely to buying works by young artists, including the Neysa McMein Purchase Awards, established in 1955 by friends of this prominent illustrator and painter; a special grant in 1955 from the New York Foundation, for works by artists not previously represented in the collection; and the Sumner Foundation Purchase Awards, designed to extend early recognition to younger artists. In 1962 the Ford Foundation inaugurated a national purchasing program by acquiring twenty-four paintings from the Annual Exhibition, of which the Museum received thirteen, mostly by artists not already in the collection. Every year the Museum itself makes one or more Juliana Force Purchases devoted to artists under thirty, in memory of Mrs. Force and her vital interest in young talent.

Due to all these factors, the Whitney's collection has an unusually large representation of the younger generation. Hence, when the New York State Council on the Arts requested an exhibition from the collection, to be circulated to museums throughout the state by the American Federation of Arts, it seemed most appropriate to concentrate on artists under forty, who are perhaps less familiar to the public than older artists. The present selection of forty works is not of course the entire representation of this age group in the collection. Any selection of a given number has to be more or less arbitrary, omitting examples of equal quality. The aim is to present a cross-section of the younger generation, chosen for diversity of viewpoints and styles, ranging all the way from realistic representation to pure abstraction.

The Whitney Museum feels privileged to participate in the program of the New York State Council on the Arts, through the exhibition and the present publication. The Council, established in 1960 by the State Legislature on Governor Rockefeller's enlightened initiative, is based on the belief, set forth in the legislative act, that "the general welfare of the people of the state will be promoted by giving further recognition to the arts as a vital aspect of our culture and heritage." By inaugurating the first extensive state project of its kind, New York has furnished an example which should be of benefit to all the states, and to the federal government. To the Council and its Chairman, Seymour H. Knox, and to its Director, John H. MacFadyen, and its Assistant Director, William Hull, we wish to extend our wishes for the continuing success of their pioneer project.

LLOYD GOODRICH, *Director*
Whitney Museum of American Art

NOTE

Dimensions in the captions are in inches; height precedes width, except for sculpture, for which the largest dimension is given. The sizes of watercolors and drawings are sight (measured within the frame or mat opening), unless otherwise noted. Except when indicated, oils are on canvas, and watercolors and drawings are on paper. Dates enclosed in parentheses are not inscribed on the works. Previous publications of the Whitney Museum of American Art have been the source of some of the artists' statements and biographical data.

David Aronson

■ *The Judges.* (1959.) Pencil. 22 x 30 3/4 (over-all). Gift of Mr. and Mrs. Chauncey Waddell.

Born Shilova, Lithuania, October 28, 1923. Came to United States in 1929. Studied at School of the Museum of Fine Arts, Boston, where he was instructor, 1942-55. Chairman of Division of Art of the School of Fine and Applied Arts at Boston University since 1955. First one-man exhibition at Niveau Gallery, New York, 1945. First prize and popular prize at Institute of Contemporary Art, Boston, 1944; purchase prize Virginia Museum of Fine Arts, 1946; traveling fellowship from School of the Museum of Fine Arts, Boston, 1946; grand prize at Boston Arts Festival, 1952 and 1954; National Institute of Arts and Letters Grant, 1958; Guggenheim Fellowship, 1960. Represented also in the collections of the Art Institute of Chicago; University of Illinois; Virginia Museum of Fine Arts; Munson-Williams-Proctor Institute, Utica, New York; Brandeis University; University of Nebraska; and others.

"This is one of many works done in recent years in expression of my interest in picturing past Talmudic and Cabalistic thought. In Talmudic Law a group of Rabbis, performing as judges, comprises a judicial body. It serves to interpret fine points of the law, handing down decisions and verdicts in a variety of disputations."

Robert Barnes

■ *Judith and Holofernes.* 1958. Oil. 72 x 84.
Sumner Foundation Purchase Award.

Born Washington, D. C., September 24, 1934. Studied at Art Institute of Chicago (B.F.A. 1956) and University of Chicago. Painted in New York 1956-61. First one-man exhibition at Allan Frumkin Gallery, Chicago, 1960. Also exhibits at Allan Frumkin Gallery, New York. Group exhibitions include Boston Arts Festival, 1959; Whitney Annual, 1961; Annual American Exhibition, 1961, and Society of Contemporary American Art Exhibition, 1961, Art Institute of Chicago; "Huit Artistes de Chicago," Galerie du Dragon, Paris, and elsewhere. Whitney Museum the first museum to acquire his work (1962). Received William and Noma Copley Foundation Award, 1961; Fulbright Grant to England, 1961 (renewed 1962). Taught at University of Indiana, summers 1960, 1961. For the last year has worked in London.

Robert Birmelin

Born Newark, New Jersey, November 7, 1933. Studied at Cooper Union Art School, 1951-54; Yale University School of Art (printmaking with Peterdi and painting with Josef Albers and Rico Lebrun), 1954-56 (B.A.), 1959-60 (M.F.A.). Assistant instructor in printmaking at Yale University School of Art, 1959-60; instructor in printmaking and drawing, Yale Summer School of Art, Norfolk, Connecticut, 1960. First one-man exhibition at Kanegis Gallery, Boston, 1960; first in New York, Stable Gallery, 1960. Represented also in the collections of Museum of Modern Art, Addison Gallery, Brooklyn Museum, Sara Roby Foundation, and others. Fulbright Grant to England, 1960-61; Rome Prize Fellowship, American Academy in Rome, 1961-62. First prize for painting at Pennsylvania Academy of the Fine Arts Annual, 1962.

"I have always painted, but from 1955 to 1960 my most successful efforts were in printmaking and drawing. This past year, I have done no prints; I have devoted myself exclusively to painting and drawing, the latter as preliminary explorations of painting ideas rather than finished pieces in themselves.

"This round table has been the subject of many of my prints, paintings and drawings. It does not stand for any constant symbol. It varies as a formal device and as an idea from work to work according to the context in which it appears."

■ *Table.* 1960. Conté Crayon. 27 1/2 x 23 1/2.

Gandy Brodie

■ *End of Winter.* 1956. Oil on composition board. 47 1/4 x 57 1/4.
Gift of Mrs. Ethel K. Schwabacher.

Born in New York, May 20, 1924. Self-taught, he was encouraged by Hans Hofmann when he began to paint. He feels that Meyer Shapiro has been the greatest influence on the development of his painting. First one-man exhibition at Kootz Gallery, New York, 1951; most recent at Durlacher Brothers, 1961. Represented also in the collections of Museum of Modern Art; Sarah Lawrence College; Phillips Collection, Washington; Chrysler Museum, Provincetown. Winner of Mark Twain Contest, 1958. Lived in Europe (Paris, Florence, Venice) in 1951 and again in 1955-56 (Italy and Spain). To Mexico in 1954. Has lived in West Townshend, Vermont, since 1958.

"I believe the painter to be an instrument expressing the untold visions of the world. Thus, his responsibility is the search for an articulate objectivity encompassing the particular visual need of his time, clarifying the visual need of the past and prophesying the art of the future.

"This painting is of the Florentine countryside and expresses the relentless winter melting to give way to a mighty spring. It asks the viewer to become one with Nature and to feel the surge of the power of the seasons changing."

Carmen Cicero

■ *Leonardo*. 1960. Oil. 64 x 80.
Gift under the Ford Foundation Purchase Program.

Born in Newark, New Jersey, August 14, 1926. Studied at Newark State Teachers College, 1947-51 (B.S., Fine Arts Major). Graduate work at Hunter College, New York, 1953, 1955. Studied with Hans Hofmann. First one-man show at Peridot Gallery, 1956. Major group exhibitions include "Young America 1957," Whitney Museum. Guggenheim Fellowship, 1957. He feels that Hans Hofmann and Robert Motherwell are the teachers who have influenced him most. Also a jazz musician. Teaches at Sarah Lawrence College and lives in Newark. Represented also in the collections of the Newark Museum, Museum of Modern Art, Toronto Museum, Brooklyn Museum, Guggenheim Museum, Nebraska Art Association, and others.

"The work is abstract. If there is a 'subject,' it is symbolic, and has the same significance as a dream."

Seymour Drumlevitch

■ *Conca d'Oro.* 1951. Oil and lacquer on composition board. 30 x 40. Gift of Mr. and Mrs. Roy R. Neuberger.

Born July 9, 1923, New York. Studied with Stuart Davis and Amédée Ozenfant at the New School for Social Research, 1941; at Cooper Union Art School, 1942-46, with Peppino Mangravite, Morris Kantor, George Picken, and Robert Gwathmey. Awarded Joseph H. Hirshhorn Fellowship, 1946; Rome Prize Fellowship, American Academy in Rome, 1950, renewal 1951; National Institute of Arts and Letters Grant, 1962. Included in "New Talent" exhibition, Museum of Modern Art, 1950. One-man show in New York, Martha Jackson Gallery, 1953, and at Albright Art Gallery, Buffalo, 1953. Represented also in the collections of Albright-Knox Art Gallery; Butler Art Institute; Brooklyn Museum; Museum of Modern Art in Haifa, Israel. Associate Professor of Art at the University of Buffalo. Lives in Buffalo, New York.

"I believe that the body of an artist's work can offer the only valid testimony of his philosophy of art. My picture was painted in Rome within one week of my return from a trip to Sicily. The forms are based on the lush and verdant growth of the 'Conca d'Oro,' the fertile plain of orange and lemon groves near Palermo."

Luis Eades

■ *Survivors.* 1959. Oil. 38 x 54.
Neysa McMein Purchase Award.

Born in Madrid, Spain, June 25, 1923. Studied in England at Bath School of Art, 1940-42; Slade School of Art, 1946-47; and Birbeck College of London University; in Mexico at the Instituto Politéchnico Nacional, 1948; and at the University of Kentucky, 1949-52. One-man exhibitions in New York at the Janet Nessler Gallery, 1958, 1961. Recent group exhibitions: Pennsylvania Academy Annual, 1961; Audubon Annual, 1962; National Academy of Design Annual, 1962; "Recent Painting USA: The Figure," Museum of Modern Art, 1962. Awards include: purchase prize, 19th Annual, Dallas Museum, 1957; purchase prize, Butler Art Institute, 1958; purchase prize, Museum of Fine Arts, Houston, 1958; Grand Regional Prize, "Art:USA, 1959"; and others. Represented also in the collections of Museum of Fine Arts, Holyoke, Massachusetts, and other museums. Taught painting at University of Texas, 1954-1961. Lives in Boulder Colorado. Teaches at University of Colorado.

"To me the representation of the human image . . . in pictorial statements about the 'human condition' is the most important, challenging and rewarding function of the painter."

Edward Giobbi

Born Waterbury, Connecticut, July 18, 1926. After military service, 1944-46, studied at Whitney School of Art, 1946; Vesper George School of Art, Boston, 1947-50; Cape Summer School of Art, Provincetown, Massachusetts, 1949-50; Art Students League, 1950-51, 1955-56; Academy of Fine Arts, Florence, Italy, 1951-54. Lived in Boston, 1947-50, then in New York until 1960 except for two trips to Italy in 1951-54 and to Holland, Germany, Spain, France, Italy 1958-60. Memphis, Tennessee, 1960-61. First one-man exhibition in New York at Ward-Eggleston Galleries, 1951; most recent at the Contemporaries, 1961. Major group exhibitions include "Young America 1960," Whitney Museum. Represented also in the collections of Art Institute of Chicago, Baltimore Museum of Art, and elsewhere. Lives in Katonah, New York.

"This painting is a sort of review of a series of still lifes that led up to it and a glimpse of future work. The use of flat geometric planes working with the loose expressionistic areas first appeared in this painting, and it is the direction in which I am most interested at the present time."

■ *Untitled Still Life Number 16.*
1961. Oil. 75 3/4 x 60.
Gift under the Ford Foundation Purchase Program.

Joseph Glasco

Born Pauls Valley, Oklahoma, January 19, 1925. Grew up in Texas. Studied at the University of Texas, 1941-42. After service in the U.S. Air Force, 1943-45, and Infantry, 1945-46, lived in Los Angeles for two years, studying four months at the Jepson Art Institute, the Art Center School, and with Rico Lebrun. In 1948 went to Mexico City, studying at the School of Painting and Sculpture at San Miguel Allende. Studied at Art Students League, New York, for five months in 1949. First one-man show at the Perls Gallery, New York, 1950. The Museum of Modern Art acquired one of his paintings the same year. Traveled through Europe and Africa, then worked in New York until 1952. Lived in Taos, New Mexico, 1952-54; returned to New York. In "Fifteen Americans" exhibition, Museum of Modern Art, 1952; "The New Decade," Whitney Museum, 1955. Represented also in the collections of Albright-Knox Art Gallery, Buffalo; Brooklyn Museum; Metropolitan Museum of Art; Museum of Modern Art. Lives in Dallas, Texas. Working during summer of 1962 in Holland.

■ *Portrait of a Poet.*
1951. Oil. 68 x 46.

Sidney Goodman

■ *Once Upon an Era.* 1960. Ink. 24 3/4 x 34 1/4.
Neysa McMein Purchase Award.

Born Philadelphia, January 19, 1936. Studied Philadelphia Museum School of Art, 1954-1958. Fellowship at Yale Summer School of Art, Norfolk, Connecticut, 1957. First one-man show at Terry Dintenfass Gallery, New York, 1961. Awarded watercolor prize, Pennsylvania Academy of the Fine Arts, 1961. In "Recent Painting USA: The Figure," Museum of Modern Art, 1962. Represented also in the collections of the Chicago Art Institute, Museum of Modern Art. Lives in Philadelphia and teaches at the Philadelphia Museum School of Art.

"If there is one aim in my work, it is that whatever I do should be a penetrating experience; one that will last for a long time. This drawing was one of a series of drawings and paintings that had to do with machines, automobile accidents, the conflict of man against machinery, and how we build machines to supposedly live in harmony with us which sometimes end up as monsters that consume us. To me, this drawing symbolizes all of this conflict, struggle and waste of man and what he creates."

Janet Compere Harwood

Born New York, March 2, 1934. Studied with Aida A. Whedon, Port Washington, 1948-52; at Beloit College, 1952-54; Tucker Merit Scholarship to Art Students League, 1959-60. The Whitney Museum was the first public institution to acquire her work. Has not had a one-man exhibition. Lives at Wading River, Long Island, New York.

■ *The Rising World of Waters Dark and Deep*. 1960-61. Ink. 22 1/2 x 33. Neysa McMein Purchase Award.

"My philosophy of art for myself is quite simple. I must know the tools of my medium until they are an inner part of me. I must constantly be filling the well of this inner part of me with as much knowledge as my vision will permit and my head will keep and then I must work. I work from chaos, finding order from confusion, picking, moving the work as I please until it works for me, and then it is finished. . . . I decided that since these are for myself I will please me first, and that is the only rightness I shall bother about.

"This drawing is about water and the sound of water. I think of sounds we made as children talking under water or the waterlike sounds of electronic music. A relationship to land, sky and the bottom of the water is considered. The drawing has the form of movement and light. . . . I am very interested in the idea of becoming. I think this is what movement on paper means. Nothing is set. The work is completed when it remains in motion within a given space."

Richard Hunt

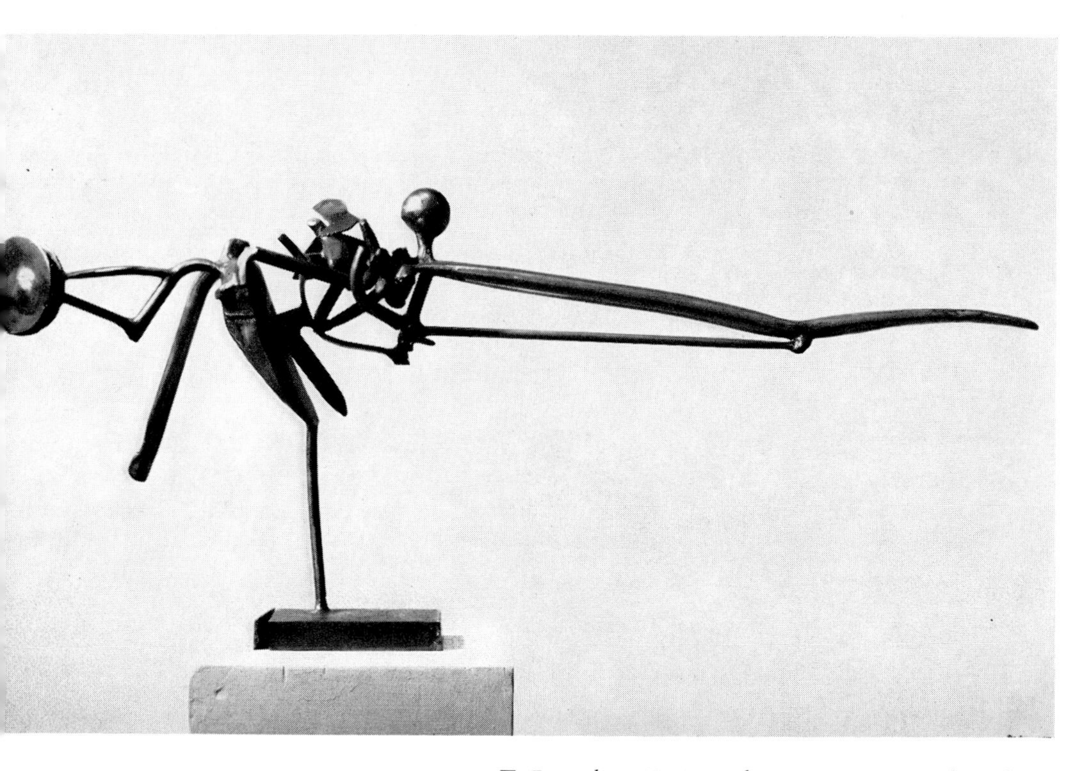

■ *Extending Horizontal Form.* (1958.) Steel. 57 long. Gift of the Friends of the Whitney Museum of American Art.

Born Chicago, September 12, 1935. Studied at the School of the Art Institute of Chicago, 1953-57, (B.A.E.). Awarded Logan Prize, 1956, and Palmer Prize, 1957, from Art Institute of Chicago. To Europe for two years, 1957-58, under James Nelson Raymond Traveling Fellowship. First one-man exhibition in New York at Alan Gallery, 1958; others there in 1960, 1962. Has exhibited in national exhibitions, including Art Institute of Chicago, Houston Museum, Pittsburgh International, Whitney Annual, Seattle World's Fair. Represented also in the collections of the Albright-Knox Art Gallery, Buffalo, New York; the Chicago Art Institute; Museum of Modern Art; and others. Lives in Chicago.

"In this sculpture my intention was to convey a feeling of a form expanding in a basically horizontal direction. Also there was an attempt to give the work an organic constitution. That is, there was an effort to effect by the undulation of forms, by twisting, curving and texturing surfaces, and through modeled joint construction, an appearance not too removed from natural forms. At the same time, I didn't wish to hide the mechanical means by which the sculpture was created. In all my work I am interested in bringing natural and mechanical, organic and geometric elements into some harmonious relation, and to hint that forms can give a sense of expansiveness if they vigorously exist in and penetrate the surrounding space."

Angelo Ippolito

Born San Arsenio, Italy, November 9, 1922. Came to New York in 1930. In U.S. Army, 1943-45. Studied at Ozenfant School of Fine Arts, 1946-47; Brooklyn Museum Art School, 1947-48. To Italy in 1948. Studied with Afro at Istituto Meschini, Rome, 1948-49. Returned to New York in 1951. First American one-man exhibition, Tanager Gallery, 1954; second, Bertha Schaefer Gallery, 1956. In Whitney Museum exhibitions "Nature in Abstraction," 1958, and "Young America 1960"; Pittsburg International, Carnegie Institute, 1961. Represented also in the collections of Munson-Williams-Proctor Institute, Utica, New York; Phillips Collection, Washington, D.C. Has taught at Cooper Union Art School; Newark School of Fine and Industrial Art; Sarah Lawrence College; and University of California, Berkeley. Presently living in New York.

"I have no direct road to painting. I have to begin somewhere. I begin with an idea . . . say an idea of sunshine on a hillside, yellow sunshine. During the process something happens . . . another color, a small change, a possibility, a discovery, dynamic relationship—then, here is reality; this is the real beginning. The crutch (the idea) isn't needed any more; the painting doesn't have to be justified. Off you go: the picture has started, and your problems begin. It all ends when you reach a place where something is happening. There has to be a drama, something dynamic, an event."

■ *Storm.* 1956. Oil. 43 x 50.
Gift of the Friends of
Whitney Museum of American Art.

Wolf Kahn

■ *Large Olive Grove.* (1957-58.) Oil. 47 1/2 x 54 3/4.
Gift of the Friends of the Whitney Museum of American Art.

Born Stuttgart, Germany, October 4, 1927. Has lived most of his life in New York. Studied at High School of Music and Art; Hofmann School of Fine Arts, 1947-49; University of Chicago, 1950-51 (B. A. in General Education). In Italy, 1957-58. Visiting Professor at University of California, Berkeley, 1960. First one-man exhibition at Hansa Gallery, New York, 1953; several since then at Grace Borgenicht Gallery and elsewhere. Included in "Young America 1960," Whitney Museum; Tokyo Biennial, 1961. First museum to acquire his work was City Art Museum of St. Louis, 1956. Fulbright Grant, 1962. Teaches at Cooper Union. Lives in New York.

"I want always to keep open a very direct relation and correspondence between my painting and everyday experience, though I'm against the simple-minded representation of everyday experience, believing rather that it can be translated into a vision and can thus liberate the imagination, not only of the artist but also that of art-lovers. I refuse to give up the specific reference which alone can particularize a picture . . . making it very definitely this thing and not that. My best paintings have been those where I know most definitely the exact place I wished to paint. I am thus not an abstract painter."

Ben Kamihira

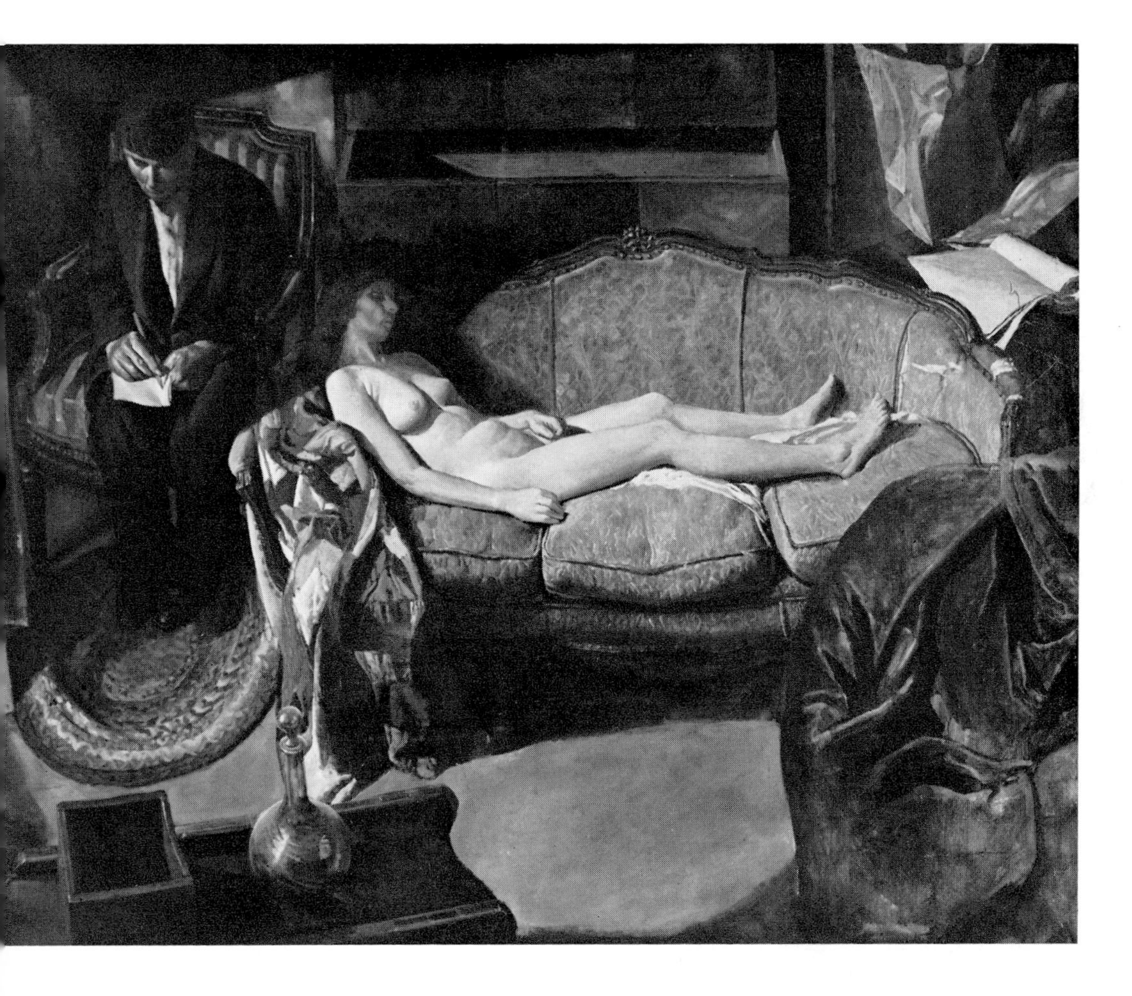

Born Yakima, Washington, March 16, 1925. Lived there until 1942, and in Jamieson, Oregon, until 1944. In Italy with U.S. Army, 1944-46. To Philadelphia in 1947, where he studied at Pennsylvania Academy of the Fine Arts, 1948-52. First one-man exhibition at Dubin Gallery, Philadelphia, 1952; others at Philadelphia Art Alliance, 1954, and Pennsylvania Academy of the Fine Arts, 1956. First one-man show in New York at Janet Nessler Gallery, 1962. Group exhibitions include "Young America 1960," Whitney Museum; "Recent Painting USA: The Figure," Museum of Modern Art, 1962. Has won numerous prizes and scholarships, including Guggenheim Fellowship, 1955 and 1956; second prize, Corcoran Gallery Biennial, 1961. Represented also in the collections of the National Academy of Design; Pennsylvania Academy of the Fine Arts; Ringling Museum, Sarasota, Florida; and others. Has lived in Primos, Pennsylvania, since 1954, except for a year in Spain, 1956-57. To be in Europe for a year from August 1962.

■ *The Couch.* (1960.) Oil. 63 x 79 1/4.
Sumner Foundation Purchase Award.

Herbert Katzman

Born Chicago, January 8, 1923. Studied at the Art Institute of Chicago, 1940-42, 1944-46. Served in U.S. Navy, 1942-44. Graduated from Art Institute of Chicago with a John Quincy Adams Travelling Fellowship. In Europe, 1947-50, spending most of his time in Paris and studying sporadically at the Académie de la Grande Chaumière, but mainly on his own. Numerous short trips to Belgium, Holland, Germany, Italy, England, and Scotland. Returned to the United States, 1950. Purchase prize, Annual American Exhibition, Art Institute of Chicago, 1951. Included in "Fifteen Americans" exhibition, Museum of Modern Art, 1952; "The New Decade," Whitney Museum, 1955; Pittsburgh International, Carnegie Institute, 1955; Venice Biennale, 1956; "Fulbright Painters," Whitney Museum, 1958. First one-man show at the Alan Gallery, New York, 1954; most recent at Terry Dintenfass Gallery, 1962. Fulbright Grant to Italy, 1956-57; National Institute of Arts and Letters Grant, 1958. Represented also in the collections of the Museum of Modern Art, and Art Institute of Chicago. Lives in New York, where he has taught at the School of Visual Arts since 1959.

■ *Two Nudes Before Japanese Screen.*
1952. Oil on composition board. 76 x 43.
Juliana Force Purchase.

David Lund

■ *Monteluco.* 1961. Oil. 56 x 76.
Gift under the Ford Foundation Purchase Program.

Born New York, October 16, 1925. Studied at Queens College, 1944-48 (B.A.); New York University, School of Education, 1948-50. Worked as textile designer, 1952-56; since then as instructor at Cooper Union Art School. Two years in Italy on Fulbright Grants, 1957-59. One-man exhibitions in New York at Grand Central Moderns, 1954; Grace Borgenicht Gallery, 1960. In "Fulbright Painters," 1958, "Young America 1960," Whitney Museum. Represented also in the collection of Toronto Art Gallery. Lives in New York.

"I spent a number of years in work that derived from Cézanne and Analytical Cubism. Gradually my focus shifted to artists whose work possessed a strong poetic or surrealist undertone. During this time, my painting evolved toward a more organic and open base. As I clarified my forms, they tended to project a deeper space, inclining into it like the planes of a landscape. Painters such as Matta, Okada, and Corbett pointed the way. The turning point came in work I did in Rome (1957-59). Since then, I have been occupied in the exploration of possibilities that first presented themselves in that body of work.

"Monteluco is a mountain in Umbria which overlooks the valley of Spoleto and the surrounding countryside. It acts as the center of that space, with wave after wave of land fanning out from it. At its top, I became the focus of that action, much as if the axis of the mountain passed through my eye, channeling the landscapes radiating substance back into myself. Within I found another vantage point . . . this one not in Umbria, having no geographic source. From it came the painting."

Marcia Marcus

Born New York, January 11, 1928. Studied at New York University, 1943-47 (B.A.); Cooper Union Art School, 1950-52; Art Students League, 1954. First one-man exhibition at March Gallery, 1957; others at Delancey Street Museum, 1960; Cober Gallery, 1961. Group exhibitions include "Young America 1960," Whitney Museum; Pennsylvania Academy Annual, 1962. Fulbright Grant to France for 1962-63. Whitney Museum the first public institution to acquire her work. Lives in New York.

"I would say that generally speaking I have never ignored what, for want of a better word, is usually called subject. I prefer object, since the subject of a painting to me is the painting, the object being merely the device through which the painting takes place and therefore no more important in a so-called figurative painting than in a non-objective or abstract one.

"The work of 1954-57, which was much freer and perhaps influenced by abstract expressionism, seems to me now, aside from whatever intrinsic value the paintings have, to be a way of reapproaching with more confidence the restrained style which seems closer to my nature. Rather than state an aim in my work I would say that a particular arrangement of choice of objects appeals to me because it has inherent in it a problem which is necessary for me to work with at the particular time at which it is chosen."

■ *Seated Self Portrait.* 1960. Oil. 54 x 50.
Neysa McMein Purchase Award.

Richard Mayhew

■ *Morning Bush.* 1960. Oil. 39 3/4 x 49 3/4.
Gift under the Ford Foundation Purchase Program.

Born Amityville, Long Island, New York, April 3, 1924. Studied at Brooklyn Museum Art School (with Edwin Dickinson and Reuben Tam), 1948-55. First one-man show at the Morris Gallery, 1957; three since then at the Robert Isaacson Gallery. Received John Hay Whitney Fellowship, 1958; MacDowell Colony Fellowship, 1958; Ingram Merrill Fellowship, 1960, for a year of travel and study in Europe. Recent group exhibitions include 64th American Exhibition, Chicago Art Institute; Pittsburgh International, Carnegie Institute; Whitney Annual—all 1961. Represented also in the collection of the Olsen Foundation, Connecticut. Lives in New York.

"I am seeking to interpret that moment of human response to nature which is not a tangible element, although I feel the association with the visual form is necessary to retain the mood. I paint not a tree or a figure but the moods. I don't work directly from subject matter, only from memory of my visual experience.

"Morning Bush *was painted in late 1960. The painting, like all my paintings, are emotional experiences with nature; visual memories that return in the course of painting which are not always planned prior to my approach to the canvas.* Morning Bush *is a strong image in a white morning light, the freshness of a new day."*

Sam Middleton

Born New York, April 2, 1927. Educated in public schools; self-taught as an artist. Scholarship to Instituto Allende, Mexico, 1956. Has traveled widely: to England, 1950; Germany, 1951; South America, 1952; Japan, 1953; Italy, 1954-55; Mexico, 1955-57 and 1959; Spain, 1959-60; Sweden, 1960-61; Denmark, 1961; Holland, 1962. First one-man exhibition at Galeria Excelsior, Mexico, 1957; others at Contemporary Arts, New York, and in New Orleans, Madrid, Stockholm, Copenhagen, Rotterdam, Munich, Cologne. Group exhibitions include: Corcoran Gallery of Art, Washington, D.C., 1958; the University of Illinois Biennial, 1959; "Young America 1960," Whitney Museum. John Hay Whitney Fellowship, 1959, and several other awards.

"Aside from always drawing and making things, such as models of boats and planes or soap carvings at community centers . . . as a child, my head and heart turned seriously towards painting around 1947-48. My first important break was my first scholarship award by Instituto Allende in Mexico, 1956."

■ *Out Chorus.* 1960.
Collage on composition board. 29 3/4 x 36.
Gift under the Ford Foundation
Purchase Program.

Joan Mitchell

Born Chicago, February 12, 1926. Studied at Smith College, 1942-44, and at Art Institute of Chicago, (B.F.A.), 1944-47. To France on Art Institute Traveling Fellowship, 1948-49. Columbia University and New York University (M.F.A.), 1950. First one-man exhibition, St. Paul, Minnesota, 1950; first one-man show in New York at the New Gallery, 1951; others at the Stable Gallery; Massachusetts Institute of Technology, 1962; Southern Illinois University, 1961; and elsewhere. Group exhibitions include the Pittsburgh International, Carnegie Institute, 1955, 1958, 1961; "Nature in Abstraction," 1958, and Whitney Annuals, 1951, 1955, 1957, 1959, 1961; São Paulo Biennial, 1959; Seattle World's Fair, 1962. Represented also in the collections of the Albright-Knox Art Gallery, Buffalo; Art Institute of Chicago; Walker Art Center, Minneapolis; Museum of Modern Art; Phillips Collection, Washington, D.C.; and the Kunsthalle, Basel, Switzerland. Lives in New York and Paris.

"My paintings are titled after they are finished. I paint from remembered landscapes that I carry with me—and remembered feelings of them, which of course become transformed. I could certainly never mirror nature. I would like more to paint what it leaves me with."

■ *Hemlock.* (1956.) Oil. 91 x 80.
Gift of the Friends of
the Whitney Museum of American Art.

Henry Niese

Born in New Jersey, October 11, 1924. Studied at Cooper Union Art School; Académie de la Grande Chaumière, Paris, 1954; Columbia University (B.F. A. 1955). Lived in New York 1947; in Montclair, New Jersey, 1948-49, 1952-55; since then in Hackettstown, New Jersey. Pulitzer Traveling Scholarship, 1954. Emily Lowe Award, 1954. Fourth prize, Corcoran Gallery Biennial, Washington, D.C., 1955. Grant from National Institute of Arts and Letters, 1958. Represented in "Young America 1960," Whitney Museum. Photographer and illustrator for English magazines on an automobile trip from London to New Zealand in 1950. Taught Brooklyn Museum Art School, 1951-55; Newark Museum, 1952-55; Summit Art Association. First one-man exhibition in New York at Gallery G, 1957. Represented also in the collection of the Corcoran Gallery of Art, and elsewhere.

"Most of my paintings are inspired by a fragment of reality such as a piece of furniture or a tree—but the major part of the work is an imaginary, formal invention.

"My aim is to paint pictures that are technically sound, combining intuitive and inventive freedom with the discipline that is necessary for a maximum esthetic and expressive impact, and with values that transcend the surface qualities of the work."

■ *The Ambry.* (1955.)
Oil on composition board. 66 x 48.
Gift of The Sumner Foundation for the Arts.

Arthur Okamura

Born Long Beach, California, February 24, 1932. Studied at School of the Art Institute of Chicago, 1950-54; Yale University Summer Art School, 1954; University of Chicago, 1951, 1953, 1957. In 1955 to France, Spain, Mallorca, and North Africa on travel fellowship awarded by Art Institute of Chicago. One-man exhibitions in California at Santa Barbara Museum of Art, 1958; Oakland Museum of Art, 1959. First one-man show in New York at Feingarten Galleries, 1960. Group exhibitions include "West Coast Painters," circulated in Germany by the U.S. Information Agency; Whitney Annual, 1961; University of Illinois, 1959 (purchase prize), 1961. Represented also in the collections of the Art Institute of Chicago, San Francisco Museum of Art, University of Illinois, Phoenix Art Museum, and others. Lives in Bolinas, California.

"I am primarily interested in presenting, through craftsmanship, a thing of suggestion. By this I mean the subject is felt through the way it is painted or drawn—one becoming the other.

"The subject of this painting was influenced by the area in which I live—ocean, mountains, woods, plains, valleys. The painting was one of the first of slight alteration in style, mood, etc., frankly and mainly from the reading of Van Gogh's letters. I paint in my studio but walk around the area looking, and retaining images which intrigue and lead to paintings. Some sketches are done on location but the paintings are all done in the studio."

■ *Fog in the Valley.* 1961. Oil. 49 x 37.
Gift of Walter Beardsley.

Robert Andrew Parker

■ *Marseilles, Night.* 1955.
Watercolor and ink.
28 1/2 x 17 1/4 (over-all).
Gift of the New York Foundation.

Born Norfolk, Virginia, May 14, 1927. Lived in Detroit, St. Louis, New Mexico, Seattle, 1928-43. In U.S. Army Air Force, 1943-46. To Chicago, 1946. Studied at Art Institute of Chicago (B.A.E.) 1948-52; Skowhegan School of Painting, summer 1952, and with Peter Grippe, Atelier 17, New York, 1952-53. First one-man exhibition at Roko Gallery, 1954. Several others since then in New York, Chicago, Boston; most recent at World House Galleries, 1961. In "Young America," Whitney Museum, 1957. Made drawings for Metro-Goldwyn-Mayer film *Lust for Life* in France and Holland, 1955. Represented also in collections of Museum of Modern Art; North Carolina Museum of Art, Raleigh. Taught at New York School for the Deaf, 1952-55, at Pleasantville Junior High School, New York. Now teaching at School of the Visual Arts, New York. Lives in Carmel, New York.

"About the first two years of school, my work was pretty much the same in subject—figures and still lifes. Then around 1951 I made a lithograph of a First World War pilot, and since then I've alternated between landscapes, etc., and things like that pilot—battles, soldiers, etc. Before 1951 I thought I had to keep my interest in that kind of thing separate from painting, but now if I get tired of one thing I work on the other, and it seems to help. As to style, it hasn't seemed to change much since 1948 . . . some of the painters I admired then I still do: Charles Demuth, Vermeer, Piero della Francesca, Paolo Uccello, G. B. Tiepolo."

James Phillips

■ *Woman with Flowers.* 1955. Oil. 17 x 21.
Neysa McMein Purchase Award.

Born Black River Falls, Wisconsin, August 11, 1929. Won scholarship in high school to Layton Art School, Milwaukee, 1947-48. University of Wisconsin (B.S.) 1949-52; Art Students League, New York, and Académie de la Grande Chaumière, Paris. Fellowship, Huntington Hartford Foundation, 1954-55. Returned to Europe, 1959-62. In Paris on Fulbright Fellowship, 1955-57. Has worked at various times as warehouse laborer, illustrator for Army, Red Cross mobile blood unit truck driver, assistant to a highway construction engineer, gag writer, airline reservationist, and sidewalk portrait painter. Has exhibited at Gallery G, most recently in 1960. Represented in "Young America 1957," "Fulbright Painters," 1958, Whitney Museum. Also in the collection of the Art Institute of Chicago. Lives in Black River Falls, Wisconsin.

"I prefer calling my present trend Poetic Realism, if it must be named. My aim is to create a visual poetic syntax; to fix the truth of the object in its passage of being—the related moment of place and object. My approach is dictated by this aim, varying as the painting derives from the memory of a moment seen, a photographic image, the vision of a situation desired."

Walter Plate

■ *Composition.* 1954. Oil on composition board. 48 x 70.
Gift of Mr. and Mrs. Jacob M. Kaplan.

Born Woodhaven, New York, June 9, 1925. Lived Long Island and New York until service with U.S. Marines, 1943-46. Studied Grand Central School of Art, 1942; Ecole des Beaux-Arts, Académie de la Grande Chaumière, and with Fernand Léger, Paris, 1947-50; Art Students League, 1952. Guest lecturer at University of Southern Illinois, 1961-62; instructor Art Students League Summer School, Woodstock, New York, since 1960. One-man exhibition, Ganso Gallery, 1954. Received Woodstock Foundation Award, 1954. Group exhibitions include Pittsburgh International, Carnegie Institute, 1955; Whitney Museum exhibitions, "Young America 1957," and "Nature in Abstraction," 1958; Corcoran Gallery Biennial, Washington, D.C., 1959 (first prize); University of Illinois Biennial, 1959. Has lived in Woodstock, New York, since 1950.

Robert Rauschenberg

Born Port Arthur, Texas, October 22, 1925. In U.S. Navy. Studied at Kansas City Art Institute, Académie Julian, Paris, 1947; with Josef Albers at Black Mountain College, North Carolina, 1948-49; with Vaclav Vytlacil and Morris Kantor at Art Students League, 1949-50. Resident artist Black Mountain College, summer 1952. Travel in Italy and North Africa, 1952-53. Stage and costume designer for Merce Cunningham Dance Company since around 1951, and for Paul Taylor. First one-man show in New York at Stable Gallery, 1953. Group exhibitions include Pittsburgh International, Carnegie Institute, 1958, 1961; "Documenta II," Kassel, Germany, 1959; São Paulo Biennial, 1959; "Sixteen Americans," 1959, and "The Art of Assemblage," 1960, Museum of Modern Art; Exposition International du Surréalisme, Paris, 1959; Paris Biennial, 1959; Whitney Annual, 1961; Seattle World's Fair, 1962. Has lived in New York since 1953.

■ ROBERT RAUSCHENBERG.
Summer Rental, Number 2. 1960.
Oil. 70 x 54.
Gift of the Friends of the
Whitney Museum of American Art.

Dean Richardson

■ *Motorists.* 1957. Oil. 53 x 78 1/2.

Born Orange, New Jersey, November 29, 1931. Studied Rhode Island School of Design (B.F.A. 1956) and Brooklyn Museum Art School, 1956-57. Max Beckmann Memorial Scholarship, Brooklyn Museum Art School, 1956. To Europe on a Fulbright scholarship where he studied at Hochschule für Bildende Kunst, Berlin, 1957-58. First one-man exhibition at Nexus Gallery, Boston, 1958; most recent Joan Peterson Gallery, Boston, 1962. Whitney Museum first public institution to purchase his work (1960). Exhibited in "Fulbright Painters," 1958, Whitney Annual, 1959, and "Young America 1960," Whitney Museum. Second prize Providence Arts Festival, 1961. Awarded Guggenheim Fellowship, 1962. Lives Providence, Rhode Island; teaches at Rhode Island School of Design.

"I always wanted to be an artist. . . . I suppose my work began to have a more personal stamp around 1956; it began to be based more on personal reactions to things than on mannerisms. . . . This work, painted in my studio in Berlin, Germany, is based primarily on a sense of difference and isolation in a new country."

Raymond Rocklin

■ *Evocation.* (1958.)
Brass. 66 high.
Gift of the Friends of
the Whitney Museum of American Art.

Born Moodus, Connecticut, August 18, 1922. Studied electronics in Army Signal Corps, Philadelphia, 1942-43. Studied drawing at Educational Alliance Art School, 1946-49. Took up sculpture at Cooper Union Art School, 1949-51. On scholarships to Skowhegan School of Painting and Sculpture, summer 1951, and to Brooklyn Museum Art School, 1951-52. To Italy on Fulbright Grant, 1952-53. Yaddo Grant, 1956. One-man exhibition, Tanager Gallery, 1956; at Bertha Schaefer Gallery, 1958, 1960; Dilexi Gallery, San Francisco, 1960. Represented in "Young America 1957," Whitney Museum. Has shown in group exhibitions at University of Illinois, 1959; University of Michigan, 1960; New School, 1961; and elsewhere. Taught sculpture at American University, Washington, D.C., 1956; University of California, Berkeley, 1959-60. Lives in New York.

"When I left Italy I never dreamed how much of the Baroque manner went with me.... I was disappointed in the Italian Baroque—for my modern temperament it was too tame, too theatrical, too literal, too weak, too solid and too conservative. But instinctively I loved the life force behind the Baroque fountains, buildings and sculpture of Italy.
"All this made me feel that the Baroque never reached its final culmination and I envisioned the marvelous potentialities of a new Baroque style. I wanted it to swirl heavenwards, to curl and lose itself within, to thunder light and shade, to breathe more of space and to thrust itself into infinity. It is all this that I now strive to create in my own work."

Sarai Sherman

Born Philadelphia, September 2, 1922. Studied at Temple University, 1939-44; Barnes Foundation, Merion, Pennsylvania, 1939-41; University of Iowa, 1944-45. Has traveled and lived in Mexico and Europe. Pepsi-Cola Opportunity Fellowship, 1946. First one-man show at Laurel Gallery, New York, 1950; others at A.C.A. Gallery, New York, 1951, 1955, 1958, 1960; and in Rome, 1955, and Milan, 1961. To Italy under Fulbright Grant in painting, 1952-53, renewed 1953-54. Has exhibited in group shows at the Pennsylvania Academy of the Fine Arts, Whitney Museum, Brooklyn Museum, Art Institute of Chicago, California Palace of the Legion of Honor, University of Illinois, National Institute of Arts and Letters, San Francisco Museum, and others. Represented in "Fulbright Painters," Whitney Museum, 1958. Represented also in the collections of the Museum of Modern Art; Galleria d'Arte Moderna, Rome; Tel Aviv Museum, Israel; Chrysler Museum, Provincetown, Massachusetts. Lives in New York.

"Painting, to me, is the search of a plastic means to express the interplay and infinite ramifications of man's vision in the total sense."

■ *The Centaurs.* (1959.) Oil. 54 x 56.
Gift of Dr. and Mrs. Frank Ross De Luca.

Jack Squier

Born Dixon, Illinois, February 27, 1927. To Elwood, Indiana, 1938. Served in U.S. Navy Air Corps, 1945-47. Studied at Indiana University, 1947-50 (B.S., Business and Art major), and with Robert Laurent at Cornell University, 1950-52 (M.F.A., Sculpture major). Spent summers of 1949-51 in Ogunquit, Maine, teaching sculpture at Ogunquit School of Painting and Sculpture. One-man exhibition, Alan Gallery, 1956, others there in 1959, 1962. One-man shows at Cornell University, 1952, 1957. Has exhibited in group shows at Whitney Museum ("Young America 1960"); Museum of Modern Art; Art Institute of Chicago; Museum of Fine Arts, Houston; Addison Gallery, Andover, Massachusetts; John Herron Art Institute, Indianapolis; and the Brussels World's Fair. The Whitney Museum was the first museum to acquire his work. Assistant Professor of Art at Cornell University. Lives in Ithaca, New York.

■ *Oracle*. 1958. Bronze. 29 1/2 high.
Juliana Force Purchase.

Theodoros Stamos

■ THEODOROS STAMOS.
High Snow—Low Sun, II. (1957.) Oil. 53 1/2 x 97 1/2.
Gift of the Friends of the
Whitney Museum of American Art.
See Frontispiece

Born New York, December 31, 1922. Left high school before graduating to work for a living; at the same time began to paint. Studied sculpture at the American Artists School, 1936-39, then turned seriously to painting as a career. Worked in the West and in British Columbia, 1947-48; in France, Italy and Greece, 1948-49. First one-man show in New York at the Wakefield Gallery, 1943. Has had eighteen one-man exhibitions, both here and abroad. Included in "The New Decade" exhibition, Whitney Museum, 1955. Has exhibited widely in major group shows, most recently in Pittsburgh International, Carnegie Institute, 1961; University of Illinois Biennial, 1961; American Exhibition, Art Institute of Chicago, 1961, 1962; Seattle World's Fair, 1962. Represented also in the collections of the Metropolitan Museum of Art; Museum of Modern Art; Albright-Knox Art Gallery, Buffalo; Walker Art Center, Minneapolis; Wadsworth Atheneum, Hartford; Tel Aviv Museum, Israel; and others. Tiffany Fellowship, 1951; National Institute of Arts and Letters Grant, 1956. Teaches at the Art Students League. Lives in New York City and East Marion, Long Island.

"What prompted High Snow—Low Sun *was a series I had begun called* The Sun Path *through another group called* The Day of the Two Suns. *The whole combined series evolved from thoughts of the solstice. As I worked, things which a painter knows about picture-making began automatically to take their rightful place in controlling the abstract arrangement, the distribution of form and color on the canvas, but always retaining one thing above all, the idea."*

Richard Stankiewicz

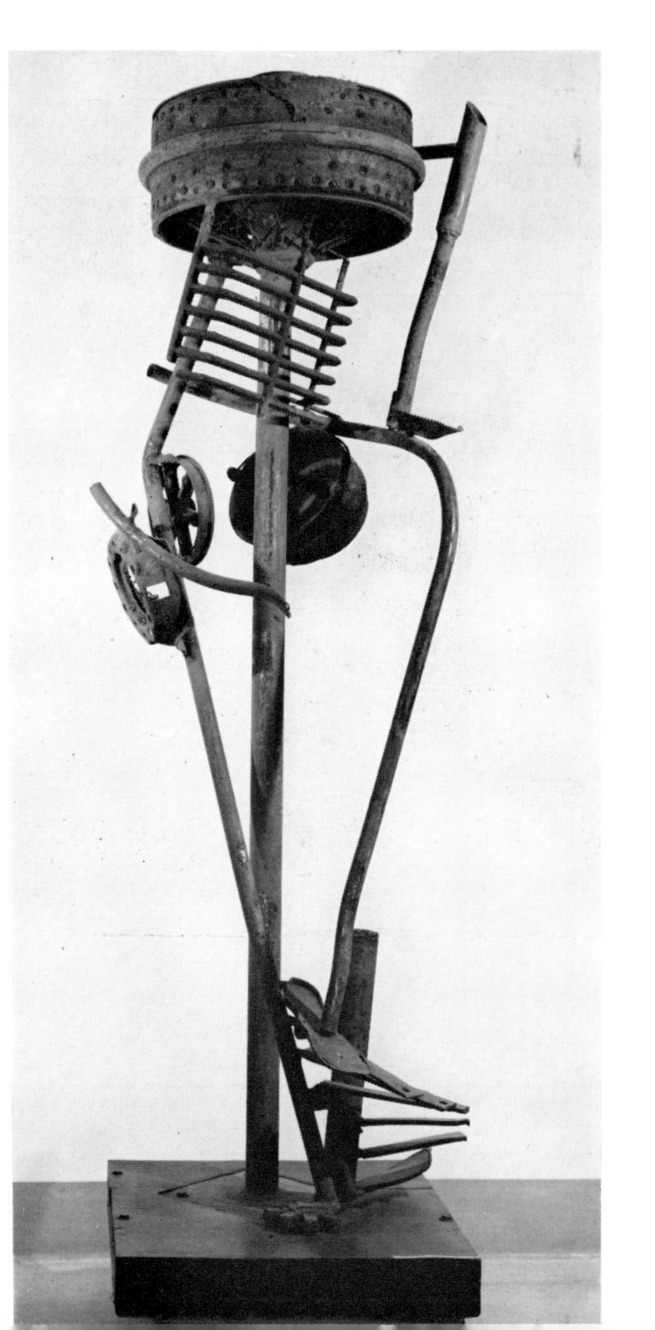

■ *Kabuki Dancer.* (1956.)
Steel and cast iron. 80 1/4 high.
Gift of the Friends of the
Whitney Museum of American Art.

Born Philadelphia, October 18, 1922. Grew up in Detroit. In U.S. Navy, 1941-47. Studied in New York at Hans Hofmann School of Fine Arts, 1948-50; in Paris for brief period at Atelier Fernand Léger, 1950, then with Ossip Zadkine, 1950-51. Returned to New York in 1951 where he has lived since. A founder of the Hansa Gallery, 1951; one-man exhibitions there, 1952-56; since then at the Stable Gallery. Since 1953 in major group exhibitions in New York, Philadelphia, Chicago, Denver, Minneapolis, Houston, Los Angeles, Pittsburgh, and elsewhere, including "Young America 1957," Whitney Museum; Venice Biennale, 1958; São Paulo Biennial 1961; and Seattle World's Fair, 1962. Represented also in the collections of Albright-Knox Art Gallery, Buffalo; Museum of Modern Art; and elsewhere. Lives in New York.

"I pursued painting until I entered the Hofmann School, where . . . I began to give more and more time to sculpture. By the time I had got to Paris and Zadkine, I was making sculpture exclusively. After some rather unsatisfying carving and modelling, I began to make terracotta constructions of the so-called open kind, which tendency soon proved too demanding on the material. Turning to wire and plaster coated wire, I continued the light, constructed kind of work which eventually proved that technique inadequate and led to the adoption of the welding tools. The use of discarded metals and machine parts followed the perception that frequently ready-made forms, properly used, are more provocative than invented effects. Also visual puns, mechanical analogies and organic resemblances in machinery provide a large and evocative vocabulary for sculpture."

James Strombotne

Born Watertown, South Dakota, October 30, 1934. To California in 1940. Studied at Pomona College (B.A., 1956) and at Claremont Graduate School (M.F.A.). In Italy on a Honnold Travelling Fellowship, 1956-57. First one-man exhibitions at Studio 44, San Francisco, and Coronet-Louvre Gallery, Los Angeles, 1956; eight others since then, including those as Frank Perls Gallery, Los Angeles; University of California at Riverside; Pasadena Art Museum. In group exhibitions at the Pennsylvania Academy of the Fine Arts; Ringling Museum, Sarasota, Florida; Whitney Museum (Annuals 1959, 1961, "Young America 1960"), University of Illinois; San Francisco Museum of Art; Baltimore Museum of Art; City Art Museum, St. Louis; and others. Represented also in the collections of City Art Museum, St. Louis; Pomona College; Scripps College. Has taught in the Extension Services of the University of California, Los Angeles, and the University of California at Riverside. Lives in Claremont, California.

"For me there must be mystery, power and beauty in my work or it has no meaning."

■ JAMES STROMBOTNE. *The Group*. 1960. Oil. 48 x 60.
Juliana Force Purchase.

Hugh Townley

Born Lafayette, Indiana, February 6, 1923. Grew up in Indiana, South Carolina and Wisconsin. U.S. Air Force photographer, later Army Medical corpsman, 1941-45. University of Wisconsin (anthropology and applied art), 1946-48. Studied with Ossip Zadkine, Paris, 1948-49, followed by a year of independent study at The Hague, and a year in London studying mural design with Victor Pasmore at the London County Council School of Arts and Crafts. Attended summer session, Massachusetts Institute of Technology, 1956. First one-man exhibition at Galerie Apollinaire, London, 1951. Major group exhibitions include "New Talent," Museum of Modern Art, 1955; "Young America 1957," Whitney Museum; Pittsburgh International, Carnegie Institute, 1958; University of Illinois Biennial, 1961. Represented also in the collections of San Francisco Museum of Art; Milwaukee Art Institute; Addison Gallery; Munson-Williams-Proctor Institute, Utica, New York; Fogg Museum, Harvard University. Has taught at Layton School of Art, Milwaukee, Wisconsin; Beloit College, Beloit, Wisconsin; Boston University. Presently living in Providence, Rhode Island, where he teaches at Brown University.

■ *Golem.* (1956.) Maple, walnut, ebano, and amaranth. 40 high. Gift of the New York Foundation.

Elbert Weinberg

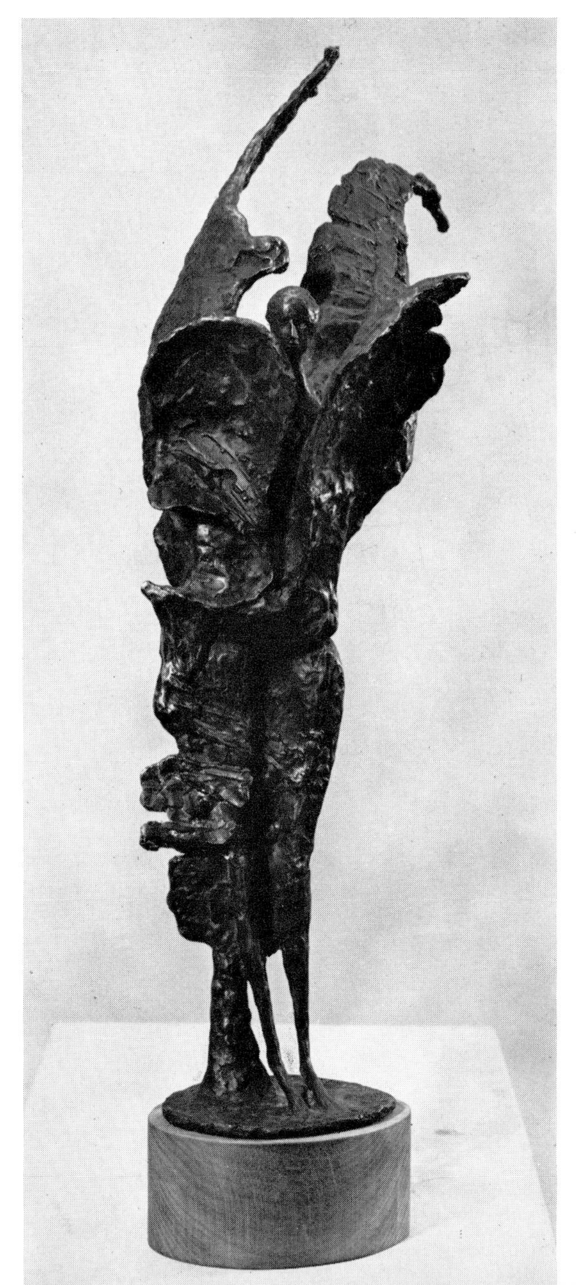

■ *Angel of Death.* (1957-58.)
Bronze. 25 high.

Born Hartford, Connecticut, May 27, 1928. Studied with Henry Kreis, Hartford Art School, 1946-48; with Waldemar Raemisch and Gilbert Franklin, Rhode Island School of Design (B.F.A.), 1948-51; Yale (M.F.A.), 1953-55. First one-man exhibition, Art Center, Providence, Rhode Island, 1951; honorable mention, Italian Division Unknown Political Prisoner Competition, 1953; Progressive Architecture Award, 1954; Guggenheim Fellowship, 1959. Included in Whitney Museum exhibition "Young America 1957." One-man shows at Grace Borgenicht Gallery, New York, 1959, 1962. Represented also in the collections of the Museum of Modern Art; Jewish Museum; Museum of the Rhode Island School of Design, Providence, Rhode Island; Wadsworth Atheneum, Hartford, Connecticut; Addison Gallery. Has taught at Cooper Union Art School. Presently living and working in Rome.

"From those early days with Henry Kreis, work was with the figure in a German tradition keynoted by Barlach and mellowed by Marcks. It continued and developed under Waldemar Raemisch through 1951. I am indebted to him for showing me what it means to be an artist; no finer teacher could I have found, no better friend. In Europe I was exposed to other directions, the painter Norman Rubington being a great influence towards semi-abstraction. The English section of the 1952 Biennale in Venice did the rest. Butler and especially Armitage intrigued me, Moore cleared the way, while the Egyptians and pre-Columbians had provided the bedrock. Fazzini is there in reapplication to craft and the unexpected twist, while Marini provided the assurance that the figure was still a vigorous affair."

William T. Wiley

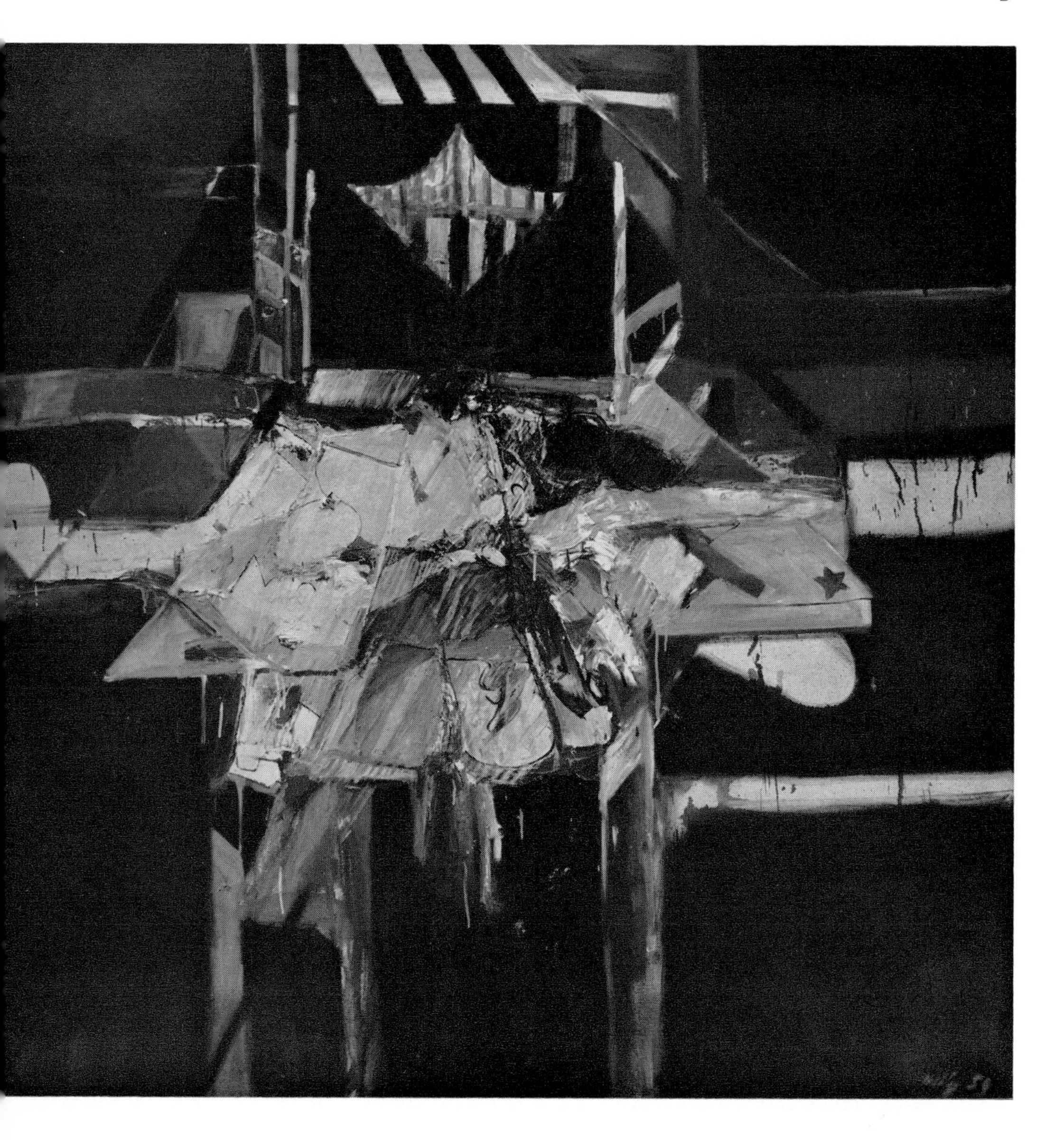

Born Bedford, Indiana, October 21, 1937. Most of childhood spent in Washington State. Attended California School of Fine Arts, 1956-1960 (B.A.). Now working toward M.F.A. degree at San Francisco Art Institute. First one-man show in New York at the Staempfli Gallery, 1962. Group exhibitions include "Young America 1960," Whitney Museum; Annual Exhibition of Painting and Sculpture, Art Institute of Chicago, 1961, 1962; University of Illinois Biennial, 1961; Pittsburgh International, Carnegie Institute, 1961; and others. Represented also in the collection of the San Francisco Museum of Art. Lives in Mill Valley, California.

"I am painting the symbols of the things I know best. I have started with the obvious, which I hope to evolve into the more subtle language of the things I see and love. . . . This was the third in a series of paintings involving American symbols—stars, shields, etc. This came about through a sudden interest in the country I was living in but was not seeing or painting. Until this time contemporary Eastern and European art had been a main interest. . . . The ideas that are present in Time Table *evolved from the schedule of clocks and disarrayed ideas that had been heaped upon my table, while going to school and trying to find the time to do what I wanted most."*

■ *Time Table.* 1959. Oil. 66 x 67.
Juliana Force Purchase.

James Wines

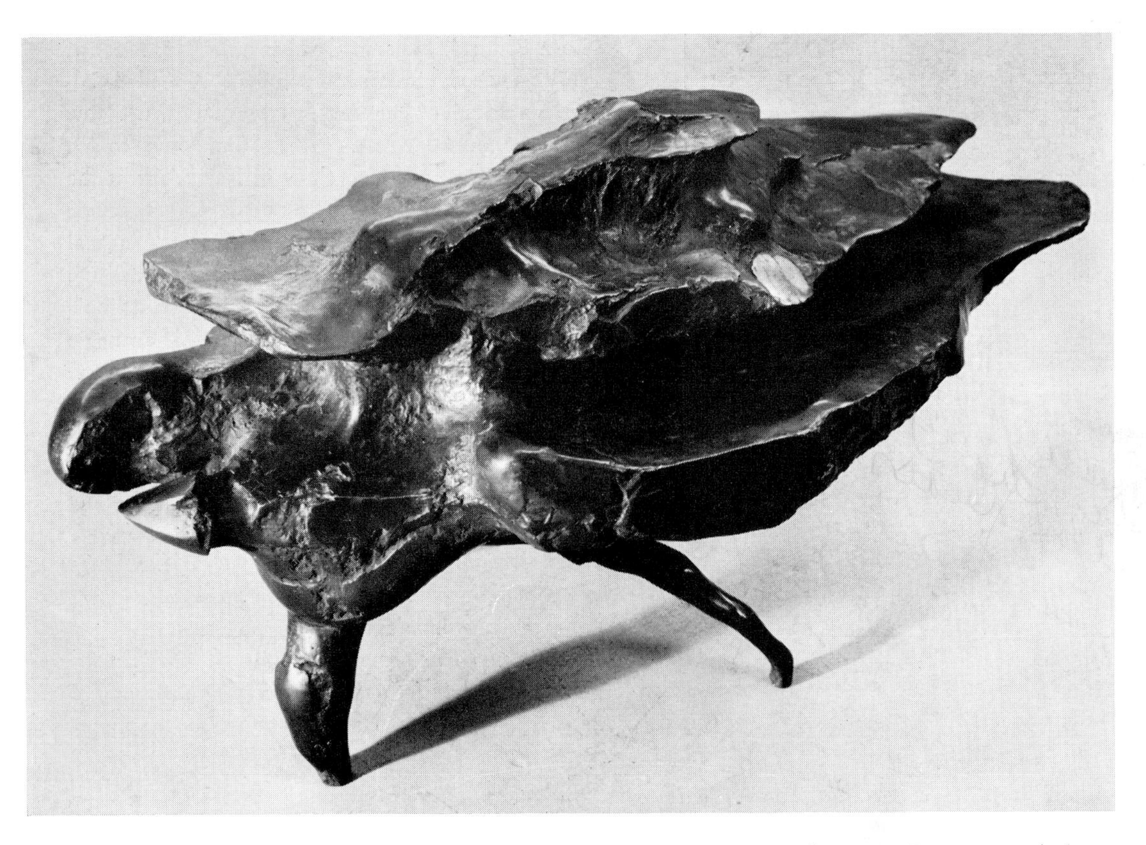

■ *Monad, I.* 1960. Bronze. 53 1/2 long.
Gift of the Friends of the Whitney Museum of American Art.

Born Oak Park, Illinois, June 27, 1932. Studied at Syracuse University, 1950-55 (B.A.), working under Ivan Mestrovic, 1954-55. Travel in Spain, France, Italy, Turkey, and Greece, 1956-58. One-man exhibitions at Syracuse Museum of Art, 1954; Baltimore Museum of Art, 1958, and at dealers in Chicago, Los Angeles and Rome. First one-man show in New York at Fine Arts Associates, 1960; most recent at Gerson Gallery, 1961. Group exhibitions include Whitney Annual, 1958, "Young America 1960," Whitney Museum; "Recent Sculpture USA," 1959, Museum of Modern Art; University of Illinois Biennial, 1959; Annual American Exhibition, Art Institute of Chicago, 1960; Pittsburgh International, Carnegie Institute, 1961. The Whitney Museum first museum to acquire his work (1960). Guggenheim Fellowship, 1962. Lives in Rome.

"Monad I *is part of a recent series of works inspired by rock and organic shapes. The title and inspiration of the piece come from the philosophical term 'monad,' meaning an individual elementary being physical or spiritual in nature reflecting within itself the whole universe. I am concerned in my work now in finding images, preferably monolithic and simple, on which I can build a powerful iconography.*"

Jack Wolfe

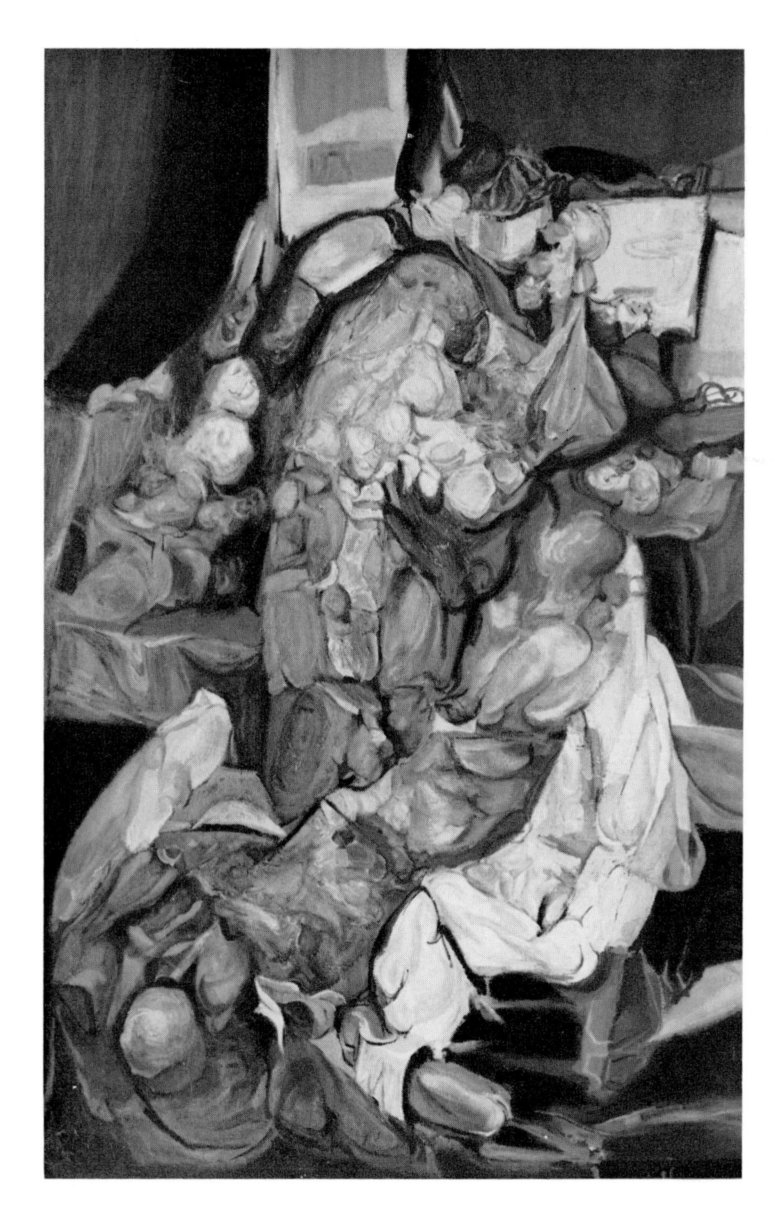

Born Omaha, Nebraska, January 14, 1924. Lived for a time in Brockton, Massachusetts, then in Boston, 1947-51. Studied Rhode Island School of Design, 1942-43; School of the Boston Museum of Fine Arts, 1945-49. Traveling Scholarship from School of the Boston Museum of Fine Arts, 1958-59. He worked as a restorer (with Gustav Klimann). One-man exhibitions: Margaret Brown Gallery, Boston, 1952, 1954; De Cordova Museum, Lincoln, Massachusetts, 1953 ,1954, 1957, 1959, 1961; Boston Museum of Fine Arts, 1961. Group exhibitions include "Young America 1957," Whitney Museum; "New Talent, USA," circulated by the American Federation of Arts, 1957; and various others. Whitney Museum first public collection to own his work. Lives in Stoughton, Massachusetts.

Wolfe describes his early work of about 1945 as "a sort of foot-dragging Boston expressionism." In 1948, he did his first abstract paintings in a system of shifting and interpenetrating forms. By the time of his initial one-man show in 1952, he had returned to a more traditional image-seeking, and he feels that his work as a restorer helped to make him conscious of "the renewal forces that an awareness of tradition gives an artist." Heavier forms more fully developed in space date from 1953-54.

■ *Downfall.* (1955.)
Oil. 72 x 46.

Thomas Yerxa

Born Oakland, California, October 20, 1923. Studied at Pennsylvania Academy of the Fine Arts, 1945-51. Attended lectures at Barnes Foundation, Merion, Pennsylvania. Awards include Cresson European Scholarship from Pennsylvania Academy, 1951; Louis Comfort Tiffany Grant, 1952; George A. Zabriskie Prize, Allied Artists of America, 1952, 1953; Thomas B. Clarke Prize, National Academy of Design, New York, 1955; Emily Lowe Award, 1958; and others. One-man shows at Janet Nessler Gallery, 1956-1962. Represented also in the collections of Pennsylvania Academy of the Fine Arts; Butler Institute of American Art, Youngstown, Ohio; National Academy of Design; Philadelphia Museum; Columbia (South Carolina) Museum; Parrish Museum, Southampton, New York. Lives in Philadelphia.

"This painting is a representational abstract, which I have tried to make function as a design without destroying its realistic content. It was executed entirely in my studio over a period of one year, during which time I worked on it sporadically using sketches from the actual scene."

■ *Deserted Warehouse.*
1958. Oil. 40 x 48.
Neysa McMein Purchase Award.